GDL

CVs for
Graduates

Time-saving books that teach specific skills to busy people, focusing on what really matters; the things that make a difference – the *essentials*.

Other books in the series include:

Succeeding at Interviews

High Powered CVs

Making Exams Easy

Making the Most of Your Time

Speak Out With Confidence

Solving Problems

Writing Successful Essays

Feeling Good for No Good Reason

Pass Your Practical Driving Test

Responding to Stress

For full details please send for a free copy of the latest catalogue.
See back cover for address.

CVs for Graduates

Gerald Higginbottom

BRACKNELL FOREST
BOROUGH COUNCIL

ESSENTIALS

Published in 2001 by
How To Books Ltd, 3 Newtec Place,
Magdalen Road, Oxford OX4 1RE, United Kingdom
Tel: (01865) 793806   Fax: (01865) 248780
email: info@howtobooks.co.uk
www.howtobooks.co.uk

British Library Cataloguing in Publication Data
A catalogue record for this book is available from
the British Library

Edited by Diana Brueton
Cover design by Shireen Nathoo Design
Produced for How To Books by Deer Park Productions
Designed and typeset by Shireen Nathoo Design
Printed and bound in Great Britain
by Bell & Bain Ltd., Glasgow

NOTE: The material contained in this book is set out in good faith for
general guidance and no liability can be accepted for loss or expense
incurred as a result of relying in particular circumstances on statements
made in the book. The laws and regulations are complex and liable to
change, and readers should check the current position with the relevant
authorities before making personal arrangements.

ESSENTIALS *is an imprint of*
How To Books

Contents

Preface

A curriculum vitae, or 'life history', is a formalised way in which job applicants summarise their suitability for employment. It will include important personal details, a summary of their skills and qualities, their employment and education records. It may also include some of the applicant's other interests and motivations.

This short book has been written for those who are coming to the end of, or have recently finished, their university course and are looking for employment. It is primarily a guide to writing your first CV. Beyond this, it is designed to help you, the reader, take stock of the assets and qualities which make you uniquely employable and to assist you to record them for your future employer.

I include a review of the things you should include in your CV. You will also consider how to read advertisements and job descriptions to extract from them information about what the employer is looking for. This will guide you as you tailor your CV accurately to the employer's needs.

There is a section dedicated to the presentation of your CV, with advice on how to set it out to best effect. Remember that if you cannot include everything on one neatly filled page of A4, fill two! Finally I have included a chapter on covering letters to help you deliver your CV to a prospective employer to your best advantage.

The sole purpose of a CV is to get an interview and should be tailored to the particular position its author is applying for. The days of having 'a CV' which might be updated from time to time are over. Expect to restructure your CV for each vacancy you apply to fill, it's worth the effort.

Gerald Higginbottom

1 Your Skills and Qualities Inventory

*If you don't know how good you are,
how will your future employer?*

The most difficult part of writing your CV
will be the section in which you describe
yourself. The first step has to be a detailed
inventory of all the things which add up to
make you unique. These are the skills,
knowledge, experiences and personal
qualities that make you very employable and
particularly suited to *this* job.

You will look at all your past experience of
work and other activities in which you
related with other people, and draw from
them examples of your own best practice.

You will also look closely at what
motivates you and how your character suits
you to the job you are to apply for. *

** You will, in effect,
be assessing your
own management
potential.*

In Chapter 2 you will see how this self

analysis is used to write your profile, the vital opening to your CV.

Is This You?

- I've got my degree now, but what has it done for me? • What qualities do managers need? • I'm not sure what to put in my about the things I think I do well. • I'm never sure if the things I've done are legitimate experience to put in my CV.

Taking Stock of Yourself

You have recently qualified with your new degree or diploma and are eager to start a new career, but there is much more to you than that. Before you take up pen or mouse to compile your CV, settle down with a pencil and list all the things which make you employable and especially suited to the job you are about to apply for.

An inventory of your skills and qualities should first consider those which are intrinsic to your character. List these under five headings:

~ your management potential

~ your interpersonal skills

~ the character traits you will bring to the job

~ your administrative skills

~ your achievements to date.

Your management potential

Graduates are appointed some way up the team structure where management skills will be expected right away, with the promise of more to come. What qualities do you have which fit you to this role?

Here are a few concepts which relate to managerial roles. Look through the list and ask yourself how many of these qualities you have. How many of them you have demonstrated already?

leadership	decision making	achieving
inspiration	delegation	initiating
motivation	assessment	monitoring
diagnosis	influencing	resolving

planning   evaluation   deciding
directing   communication   supervising

Do you have leadership potential?

Effective managers carry their team with them. There is no doubt who determines the agenda or makes the decisions, but the team knows that their leader fully accepts that the buck stops there and they are fully prepared to deal with it when it does. *

To manage effectively it is necessary to *delegate* effectively. This does not mean passing on jobs (nor the buck). It is giving a colleague the responsibility, the freedom and the authority to complete a project as agreed with you. You *initiate* the activity, *observe* its progress, *assess* the outcomes.

Can you *co-ordinate* the efforts of a group of people, *assessing* their individual strengths, *planning* a stratagem with them, *influencing* how they perceive the task and propose to go about it? Could you then *supervise* their efforts, *resolve* any conflicts that arise, help them *solve* unexpected

* Leaders inspire respect and loyalty, so the team members achieve more than they would as a group of individuals.

problems and *evaluate* the outcome?

Do you have the *communication* skills to support your other attributes: oral skills to *persuade* or *inspire* team members, writing skills to *record* decisions, progress, outcomes and to complete reports?

With these, as with the other personal qualities we will consider next, it is now your task to think of examples of *how, when* and *where* you have demonstrated these abilities. *This is crucial to compiling a successful CV.*

Interpersonal skills

Now consider your capacity to relate to others and communicate with them. It is about your ability to get the best from people by finding the balance between the stick and the carrot.

Here are a few activities that are relevant to this aspect of your working life:

inspiring	coaching	training
team building	appraisal	counselling
listening	appreciating	monitoring
evaluating	persuading	empathising

Ask yourself what opportunity you have had to demonstrate these skills. Your examples do not have to have come from your time (if any) in paid employment. The chance to show your potential as a 'good people person' can have arisen in your academic, social or sporting life: wherever you have interacted with others.

When faced with a shared problem, have you been able to inspire others to rise to the occasion? Have you engendered a team spirit that helped a group see a task through? *

Can you then persuade them to follow the joint line of action, probably training them in the skills they need to play an effective role in the joint effort?

Are you capable of monitoring the progress of the group, appreciating what is well done, coaching members who are not performing to their full potential so that at key stages you could evaluate the success of the exercise to date, appraise each member of the team, counselling them as necessary?

Of course you have not yet had the

* If members of the team met problems, could you find time and patience to listen to them, empathising with their worries but able to identify and assess their difficulties with them?

opportunity to display all of these skills, but remember which you have had success in: they go into your CV.

Your personality

We all bring our own personality to the job. This is what determines how we react to pressures of work and the challenges and rewards it offers. Analyse how you work best. Do you insist routines must be modified to meet every changing circumstance or would you rather subscribe to the principle: 'if it ain't broke, don't fix it'?

The following attributes are paired and roughly represent opposites in working philosophies. Do you recognise yourself in any of them? There is no 'right' or 'wrong' side, just different ways of responding to the problems of professional life.

It must be perfect.

                      If it works, it's all right.

It's good, it's new.

                      This is tried and tested.

I've restructured the team.

                      The old team got on well and succeeded.

Keep to the schedule.

Finish before the deadline.

I work best under pressure.

I need to allow myself time for setbacks.

I thrive on routine.

I can adapt to most situations.

I like reassurance.

I am confident and self-reliant.

I work best in a team.

I do my best work on my own.

I always expect success.

I fear the worst until it's done.

Make use of what works.

Iron out the faults.

I enjoy a challenge.

The prospect of failure worries me. *

On being a perfectionist

* Successful individuals are not all to the left or the right of any of these divides but they do know their own strengths and make best use of them.

Is it more important that what we produce is perfect, or that it performs adequately – and who determines what is an 'adequate' performance?

If our products don't reach the market place in time, at a price the customer will pay, they may be commercially valueless since they won't sell and so recoup their development and production costs. Many have found to their cost that 'perfect' was not good enough because 'adequate' sold better!

About innovation

There is a time for innovation and those who can innovate are in demand and valued. Equally there is a place for 'systems maintenance' people who can ensure that good working practices can be maintained.

Whilst most commercial and industrial organisation is centred on the team with all its inherent strengths, there are the radicals and mavericks who don't ever seem to fit into a working group but who nevertheless produce excellent results in isolation.

Thinking about yourself

All of the pairs of personality patterns above are two-edged swords. Any one in the wrong place, or to the wrong degree, can be as much a weakness as a strength. Neither the need for approval nor the ability to get on regardless of the feelings of others is, in itself, a strength or a weakness. *There is a time and place for both.*

This shows the importance of doing your inventory with the job description of the post in front of you. Can you infer what behaviour they are looking for for *this* job? Do they want a team player or an independent operator? Someone who will methodically keep to a routine and the schedule, or one who will cope well under pressure and adapt working practice to suit changing circumstances? Someone to sweep in with a new broom, or one to preserve best of current practice?

As all competitions advise, 'using your skill and judgement' determine what kind of person the employers are looking for and decide which of your characteristics best suit you to 'their' profile. By now you should have realised that you don't have 'a copy of my CV' or even 'my most recent CV'. *You have the CV which you prepared for* this *application.*

As before, write on your notepad as much

evidence as possible to support the characteristics you want to emphasise in this CV for this application. You are doing nothing in the least underhand or dishonest in trying to match your CV to the job. *

Your administrative skills

You may not be applying for a job as an administrator, but you will be expected to have administrative skills. Don't confuse 'administration' with 'clerical'; what is expected here goes beyond the storage and retrieval of information and the recording of data. It is about how capable you are of organising your own and others' workloads.

Consider the following skills which may be expected of you in your new job. Again it is unlikely that you have had the opportunity to demonstrate all of them in a working environment, but which have you shown competence in – when, where and how? Can you:

* It is important that you maximise your chances of success by highlighting the qualities you do have in light of what you believe the employer wants.

1 Allocate tasks fairly while using colleagues' particular strengths?

2 Produce balanced rotas and work schedules?

3 Prioritise the team's and your objectives?

4 Check that important minutiae are not lost for the overall view nor the main objective lost in trivial detail?

5 Ensure that work progresses in accordance with parameters laid down?

6 Monitor progress and recommend changes to effect improvements?

7 Record fully and accurately all salient information?

8 Anticipate the resources needed and see they are provided in time?

9 Prepare contingency plans to overcome problems?

Notice that all the above presuppose other skills. You cannot allocate tasks according to your colleagues' strengths unless you have evaluated their work and assessed their abilities. *You cannot record salient information if you are unable to distinguish the essential from the irrelevant.* How do you prepare contingency plans if you cannot anticipate the problems that might arise?

Note which of these skills you have managed to demonstrate. You have had a short working career so far, therefore you will look to your other activities as well as employment to find examples.

What part did you play in the organisation of group activities and presentations for your course?

Review the placements and work experiences you have had. What was your position in the staffing structure? Think about the duties this imposed upon you and the opportunities it presented to you. How did you respond?

How have you influenced the working practices of other organisations you have been part of: perhaps clubs, societies, fund raising groups or *ad hoc* committees?

Evaluating your achievements

Employers want successful people: your success is theirs. It is assumed that individuals who have once been successful will continue to be so. *

Saving money

What have you done to improve the cash flow of an organisation? You may have devised an economy that saved expense, found a cheaper source of supply or an alternative service provider. *Anything you have done in this respect will enhance your CV and your chances of an interview.*

Saving time

When rival car manufacturers in Detroit complained to Henry Ford that they could not afford to match the wages he paid, he responded by explaining that his work force spent less time walking around the factory and that 'perambulation was never a well paid activity'.

You don't need to have invented the

* An important element of your CV will be the successes you have enjoyed so far.

production line to save your employers' cash. Has the introduction of new software improved efficiency? A change in the office or workshop layout could have a similar effect to Henry Ford's innovation, as could a simple change to routine.

Systems improvement

Consider the effect of computerising a paper data base or of writing a suite of standard letters to cover the majority of routine correspondence. What would be the effect of devising a system to highlight all accounts which are more than 30 days overdue?

Have you suggested any change which has improved the efficiency of your workplace, club or group?

Team building

What effect have you had on the dynamics of any team you have been part of? Good 'team players' are not slaves to the team's objectives but are catalysts to group dynamics. What example could you quote to support an assertion that a group you have been part of has been more successful because of your inclusion?

Being supportive

Have you ever noticed that a friend or colleague was struggling with some task? Did you help them to identify the nature of the problem? Offer help or advice to overcome it?

Persevering

Instant success may not always be as great an achievement as that brought about by perseverance. Neither Robert Bruce nor his spider would have lived so long and affectionately in folk lore if the arachnid had bridged that gap at its first attempt.

Can you relate examples of how achievement only came about as a result of your perseverance? The ultimate success could be practical, a problem solved. Equally it could be a working relationship achieved with someone with whom you had got off to a bad start, or a reluctant customer who needed persuasion and reassurance to buy.

Academic success

Remember that your new qualification is a success as well. Although it is listed elsewhere in your CV as a qualification, it may be worthwhile detailing some element of it as an achievement too. Perhaps you solved a problem with a workshop technique. You may have come up with a particularly useful piece of market research or a useful new interpretation of an old set of data. *

Summary Points

★ Learn your own strengths, especially those about relating to people by examining your past employment and work experience in detail and extracting everything you have gained from them.

★ Identify and, as far as possible, quantify all your past successes.

* Every higher education course presents opportunities for originality. What did you do?

2 Personal Profiles

When I read a CV, the profile tells me more about a graduate applicant than all the other parts put together.

Regarded by some as an 'optional extra', you should see your personal profile as an essential part of your CV. You have not yet had a long career so your record of achievements in employment will be correspondingly short. Your potential is therefore not so apparent.

As you read the last chapter, you thought about the skills and aptitudes that are important to composing this paragraph about yourself. The next stage is to match *your personal inventory* to the qualities sought by your future employer.

The profile which you write will introduce you to a selector describing who and what you are. It must be honestly and objectively written, designed to create an impact and to highlight your best attributes. *

Is this you?

- I'm not really sure what a profile involves.
- I haven't written a personal profile before and don't know how to start. • I don't see the point of writing a profile, it's not like an independent reference is it? • I hate singing my own praises.

Choosing the right vocabulary

The vocabulary you use should be carefully chosen to create the right image and the language you use will be positive yet succinct. Try to avoid using 'I'.

Imagine that you want to say you can speak a second language. Would you say 'can speak French' or 'fluent in French'? Clearly 'fluent' carries extra meaning, conveying the impression that your French is better than adequate. It also does this with remarkable economy of space.

Compare the claims:

It must also take into account what the advertisement and job description suggest the employer will be looking for in making this appointment.

'I can word process using either Word or WordPerfect.'

'Competent in Word and WordPerfect.' *

Consider the words in the list below:

able	decisive
accomplished	detailed
accurate	developed
action	diplomatic
adaptable	direction
analytical	effective
articulate	efficient
benefiting (from)	enabling
capable	encouraging
committed	enterprising
communicator	enthusiastic
competitive	established
contribute	evaluative
control	excellent
conscientious	experienced
consistent	expert
constructive	flexible
conversant	facilitator
co-operative	implement

* *Clearly the latter says more and it does so using fewer words: it is more effective because it uses better vocabulary.*

influential
informed
initiating
innovative
integrate
introduce
investigative
launched
liaise
maintain
monitor
motivated
negotiate
opportunistic
organised
originate
performance
persuasive
potential
practical
prepared
prioritise
productive
promote
propose

qualified
resourceful
significant
skilled
specialist
stimulate
stable
structured
strong
successful
supportive
supervise
tactful
train(er)
transform
turn round
unite
versatile
voluntary
vision
winning
worthy

These are examples of the words that you should use to create the right impression in your profile. No doubt you can think of others more relevant to your own situation. Your next task is to combine them into telling phrases and sentences to describe you, your skills and qualities. *

Making an impact

Consider the following first sentence of the personal profile, the opening to the CV sent in by Lisa Edwards who was applying for a primary teaching post.

I have always wanted to work with children and gained much useful experience baby-sitting for my older sister before I went to college.

Does this opening to Lisa's profile create an impact? Hardly, but what impressions does it create in the mind of the reader?

1 Lisa has no real reason for wanting to *teach*, 'work with children' covers a multitude of jobs.

* *When you connect these into a succinct paragraph, try to ensure that they convey a positive note and that the principle verbs you use are in an active tense.*

2 Is she mature enough to be an effective teacher, or still the little sister?

3 Is baby-sitting her most significant experience to date or her principal motivation?

4 Why did she go to college, what did she get out of it?

These are certainly not the impressions that Lisa wanted to convey to the selection panel. You might try to reword this opening sentence for her. What would you want to achieve by it? Perhaps you would aim to convey commitment and enthusiasm:

Strongly motivated NQT with significant experience working with children prior to qualifying.

This is an improvement on the original. Try to analyse what makes it better. Note the following differences:

~ The 'I have (always)' is superfluous.

~ The use of 'strongly', 'motivated',

'significant' and 'qualifying' set a better tone.

~ Using 'NQT' (newly qualified teacher) shows a familiarity with the jargon of the profession: already a 'member of the club'.

Lisa had replied to an advertisement for a key stage 2 ('KS2') teacher in an urban primary school which suggested that a willingness to help with games would be an advantage. Her full profile, as Lisa wrote it for her CV, was as follows:

I have always wanted to work with children and gained much useful experience baby-sitting for my older sister before I went to college. As part of my BEd degree at UCE Birmingham, I did three teaching practices and enjoyed them all. On my final practice I started a recorder club which was very popular with the children. I enjoy athletics and netball and would be willing to help with PE lessons. In my spare time I like doing craft-work and play netball for the county.

As an applicant, Lisa clearly has a lot going for her, but you almost have to read between the lines to find it. Certainly she is not her own best advocate.

Creating the right impression

Put yourself in the role of teacher for a moment and 'mark' Lisa's profile above. You want to be helpful to the author, not destructive of her efforts; come up with some constructive suggestions to guide her to write a better profile, just using the information she chose to use about herself. The first sentence has already been dealt with. Ideas which come to mind include:

1 'BEd degree' is not helpful, it will be listed with her other qualifications, try to expand on the idea. Perhaps use a word like 'qualifying' and has she any KS2 experience?

2 Her university will be listed elsewhere so the name is not needed here, but references to 'urban' or 'inner city' might be useful to indicate the relevance of the schools she has experienced.

3 For the recorder club, 'started' and 'popular' might be improved upon. Try 'successfully introduced' and perhaps work in 'enthusiasm'.

4 Lisa has not made best use of her sporting talents. Where are the ideas of her own considerable skill and enthusiasm? In response to 'willingness to help with games', should we not read words like 'eager' and 'coaching'?

5 Lisa's craft work gives her the opportunity to introduce the concept of creativity.

6 Teachers aren't supposed to have 'spare time', certainly not when they are 'NQT'!

The profile Lisa could have written might have looked something like the following (QTS is 'qualified teacher status'):

Strongly motivated NQT with significant experience of working with children prior to qualifying. Three enjoyable and successful teaching practices completed in inner city primary schools at KS1 and KS2 before graduating with QTS. Creative craft worker and musician: established a flourishing recorder club in school during final practice. A keen and active athlete and games player to county standard who is eager to become involved with coaching school teams.

The final version is 25% shorter than the original and is all the crisper for it. It is also more positive in the impression it creates beyond the text. *Notice the language, for example the replacement of 'willing to' by 'eager to'.* *

* *Also note the effective presentation: justifying the text (giving a straight right hand margin as well as that on the left).*

Tailoring your profile to the job

In the last section we saw how Lisa's profile was improved by ensuring that it matched the demands of the job. This meant including details to correspond with all the requirements of the prospective employer.

Advertisement	Lisa's revised profile
Qualified teacher	NQT, graduating with QTS
for key stage 2	teaching practice at KS1 and 2
urban primary school	in inner city primary schools
willing to help with games	eager to ... teams

Before you start to write your profile, try to work out how many sources of information you should research first. You should include:

1 The job advertisement

2 The job description

3 The company profile

4 The nature of the business sector the employer works in

5 Your knowledge of and any previous
   experience in the sector.

Are there any other sources of useful
information you might investigate, perhaps
acquaintances who work for the company or
for a rival? Their marketing material may give
you a good feel for the work they do, as
would any recent media coverage you might
be able to find. Try searching through the
press (local as well as national) and trade
magazines. If you can do this from CD-ROM
copies of the publications, it will make your
search faster and more thorough.

   This done, try to match your qualifications,
experience, aptitudes and personality to their
requirements as you perceive them.

   When you write your profile, in view of
your limited experience to date, it would not
be out of place to also indicate your career
aspirations. The career path of an applicant
with some years' experience should be
apparent from their career history. In the
absence of a long career background, it is
quite in order, indeed desirable, to outline in

brief where you see yourself going. An
employer would not be impressed if it
appeared that this, perhaps your first 'real'
job, was the full extent of your ambition. *

Examples

Advertisement

Customer Services Staff

Are you speaking our language?

We are looking for a candidate of high calibre
who can excel in a multi-lingual customer
service role involving Internet-based queries.

If you can:
- converse in German, French and English,
  all at business level
- show excellent communication skills
- offer knowledge of the Internet and e-mail
- be PC literate

this can be the ideal opportunity for you to use
your skills in an exciting and challenging role. In
return we offer excellent salary and benefits.

Call Anna Smith today on 020 72★★ 61★★

** It does no harm to
establish that
although recently
qualified, you
have drive, are
ambitious and
hope, no expect,
to go far.*

Look at the requirements of the job and prioritise them from the employer's viewpoint. They appear to be:

1 Language/communication skills.

2 Internet fluency.

3 Computer literacy.

Now look at the advert again and infer what else the advertiser will be looking for in their ideal applicant. You might feel these include:

1 The ability to grasp the nature of an enquirer's problem quickly.

2 Capacity to empathise with enquirers, whose first language is not your own.

3 Stamina; call handling is very tiring. *

Note that experience of working in this capacity is not required, nor is knowledge of the nature of the employer's business.

Profile

Ambitious recent graduate of European Business Studies (2:1 Hons.), fluent in French and German at all levels. Recent experience working in commercial placement in Munich following 12 months' study at the University of Marseilles. Excellent oral and written communication skills. Fully computer literate and familiar with PC-based systems for Internet access, e-mail and word processing. Self-starting, energetic hard worker with good sense of humour and proven ability to empathise with others in three languages.

Advertisement

The specific details of the advert are clear. *

The ideal background shows that they are not really looking for a first appointee. If this would be your first post you will have to make best use of your experience to date.

Twenty-five appointments a week is five per seven-hour day; you will certainly need to be *organised* and expect to drive to your customers *before and after* your advertised hours.

'Fully structured career path' implies that they are looking for someone to *stay* with the company for an extended period, if suitable.

The company car suggests you detail your *driving experience*.

Generous commissions indicates that the basic salary is quite small. Have you the *confidence* to tackle this without a track record in sales?

There is no mention of locality. Are you willing to relocate if necessary for this job?

'OTE' are 'on target earnings', this is a target-led job and you will be *working under pressure*. Can you cope with this? If you don't

* Look for what is implied by the other information and consider how these should shape your profile.

meet your targets, you would be likely to lose more than your anticipated commission: the job could go too!

Before you work on your own profile, use this example and try to compose the ideal profile for this job.

Key skills

An alternative approach to this is to have a separate section under your profile headed 'Key Skills' in which you list the important skills you have for this job. The applicant for the call centre above could have written:

Key skills
- Fluent in social and commercial English, French and German.
- Good communication skills, written and oral.
- Familiar with Internet.
- PC literate with good IT skills.
- Highly motivated.
- Capacity to keep to demanding work schedules.
- Ability to empathise with others.

Summary Points

- Study the vocabulary list in this chapter and incorporate into your profile as many of the words from it as you can: use positive language.

- Practise writing about yourself without using 'I' or 'my' and word your profile to create maximum impact; this is your opening shot, don't miss.

- Infer what you can from the information you have about the job and then make sure that your profile describes the person they are looking for.

- Read advertisements and job descriptions with care and in detail, and ensure that your CV reflects the expertise and potential sought by the advertiser.

3 Career Profiles and Achievements

I am not as impressed by what graduates tell me they can do as by what they've already done.

You may feel that, because you are so recently qualified, you have not got a significant career record to write about. In the sense that traditional CVs are drafted, this may well be so. *You need an alternative style of presentation.*

In this chapter you will see how to extract all the worthwhile experience you have gained from your previous work activities, paid, unpaid and voluntary, to produce a record of what you have achieved. This will be more valuable to you than a record of former posts and employers. You will stress what you have gained from your exposure to a working environment. *

* You will not dwell on its brevity and in all probability its menial nature, compared with the post for which you are applying.

Is this you?

- I don't feel I've had much of a career to write about yet. • I'm worried that by taking a gap year I've lost ground in the job market. • I'm not sure what counts when it comes to 'achievements' • I did a sandwich degree but I'm not sure if the extra year was worthwhile.

Your employment record

You will have to decide whether you have had enough paid employment to feature this as a section by itself. It is most probable that this is not the best way forward for you, and your section on work experience and achievements should put the emphasis on what you have *gained* from your experience of work rather than a chronological listing of the posts you have held.

It is not usual to name your former employers in your record of employment, but you should give the title of the positions you have held and the dates. Do not give the name of a post which is peculiar to your own company's structure or has an obscure meaning.

Start with your current post if you have one, if not then your most recent. If you have had many jobs, only the most recent need to be described in depth, unless you are changing career direction back to a former interest.

For each position you mention, give a brief outline of your duties and what you *achieved* whilst in post.

A period of work experience as a data entry clerk whilst preparing for or studying towards a degree in business or computing could read:

1997   Data entry clerk
Making routine entries of
customer orders onto database.

But it does not say much for the author, especially as the post applied for will carry much more responsibility than this suggests the writer could cope with. The job title is not inspiring, 'routine' then belittles the job

and 'making' could read 'responsible for'.
The entry would be better written as:

1997
Sole responsibility for maintaining data base of customer details and orders. Liaison with despatch and invoice departments.

Main achievements
Became skilled in use of DataEase (DOS and Windows versions) and Access. Introduced improved communication channel between three key departments so cutting order turn around time by one working day.

Note the shift in emphasis from 'what I was required to do' to 'what I achieved during this time'. The use of 'main' in the title suggests that you, and the employer, got much more from your experience of 1997 than you list, but space is tight! Be prepared to expand on this outline at interview if necessary. *

* Remember, the purpose of a CV is to get you an interview, not the job.

Work experience

You may have to rely heavily on your unpaid work experience in this section. This is not a disadvantage since the experience is no less valid for not being financially rewarded. However, you may find it more difficult to claim very meaningful achievements in terms of employer benefit because of the short duration of the placement and your main reason for being there was to learn. Do not however dismiss it; just ensure that there is emphasis on *what* you learned from the experience.

Work-shadowing is an opportunity to follow a professional for a period and learn about the job by observation rather than practice. It is not easy to get experience of being a dentist or barrister before qualifying. Although the benefits of shadowing may not be so obvious as those from 'hands on' experience, they are still worth recording.

You probably learned more than you expected, whichever experience you have had. Make an inventory of your new knowledge under:

~ company structure, hierarchy and management models

~ clerical and IT systems to aid management functions

~ information storage and retrieval

~ your own interpersonal skills

~ means of communication within the business and without

~ the interfaces with client, customer, supplier, public, agencies ...

~ costing of products or services

~ marketing strategies and public relations

~ add on from here!

When you think about it, you achieved quite a bit, didn't you? *

* *When you write about these new skills and knowledge in your CV, use expressions like: 'became proficient in ...', 'acquired skills in ...' and 'gained expertise ...' as variations on the theme 'learned about'.*

Placements and sandwich degrees

If you did a vocational degree, it is to be hoped that you had the good fortune or common sense to take any option within your degree to spend extended periods on placement in industry. *The time you spent in this capacity will be invaluable in securing employment.*

When writing up this experience, you should make clear that this was an industrial placement ('professional' or 'commercial' if you prefer). It is also quite in order to quote the name of the organisation you were placed in and this is particularly so if you have spent time with a major player in the sector. You bring to any potential employer inside knowledge of the business of a competitor. Your reasons for leaving cannot be questioned, you got to the end of your placement, returned to complete your studies and are only now in the job market.

It can only help your cause if, for example, when placed with a recruitment agency your achievements included:

Became proficient in the maintenance of databases and in the matching of prospect to client.

You have spent several months receiving a sound induction and training at someone else's expense and, moreover, you now know about a (prestigious) rival's business. You could be quite an asset!

Think back to your own placement. What did you get from it? Do not ignore what may seem obvious. Lack of details here may permit the reader to infer that you could have written:

Made excellent pots of tea, learned quickly who took sugar and how much. Improved efficiency of despatch dept. by introduction of damp sponge for stamps. Accurate filing achieved.

Of course, you learned much more than this, so say just what you learned and what you achieved. Every skill you acquired, everything you learned about the trade and every piece of good practice you mastered makes you more valuable as a new employee. You will be:

~ productive more quickly

~ cheaper to train

~ able to bring in new ideas.

Your year out or gap year

If you took a 'year out' or 'gap year', that is spent a year between school and university or after university doing something totally different like travelling, ask yourself two questions:

1 Why did I do it?

2 What did I get out of it?

Any reason for taking a year out of full time education, between university and employment, or as a break before other responsibilities make it more difficult, can be valid. Explain your motive. It may be that before studying to become a product designer, you thought time working on the production line would give you a better insight into the problems you might otherwise inflict on others. You might just want to get a little more financial security from a year's work. Perhaps you had to get some of the wanderlust out of your system before settling down.

Neil had accepted a place at King's College, London to read geography before picking grapes in France, travelling overland to Egypt, Israel and the Far East, then coming home via Australia and Nepal. Inspired by the diversity of cultures he had experienced, on his return Neil gave up his geography place and studied anthropology instead. He never looked back, got a First, and is now three years into a successful and rewarding career.

Your reasons may be connected with your studies, your future career or neither. *

There are no 'wrong' reasons, but yours should be explained. After all, you are motivated by reason, not the subject of whim and passing fancy aren't you? Say 'yes'!

What you got out of your year may not be so easy to describe. You will be a stronger person, more self reliant, better motivated and more able to benefit from your experiences, past and future. You may not be fully aware of all the changes yourself. Try asking someone who knew you well before your year out how they think you have changed. Trust their judgement and commit some of their ideas to your CV draft.

Your section might read:

1998 Gap Year
Nine months with VSO in Old Calcutta mission station. Taught English in primary school and to adults in evenings. Helped at a feeding station. Have new-found respect for 'third world' peoples and better understanding of their problems. A more tolerant, yet more resilient person, my motivation is stronger than ever.

Or following a year in Australia:

1997 Year travelling in Australia
Amazing year! Climbed Ayre's Rock, dived over the Barrier Reef and spent three months persuading reluctant Australians to buy time shares on Bali – not without success! Met some great

people and learned more about life
(and myself) with each new hostel and
Greyhound bus.

Your achievements to date

This is not the time to be self-effacing.
Whatever you have achieved so far, now is
the time to describe it. There is great
advantage to be gained by quantifying any
achievement that is quantifiable. This may be
an amount of time saved in a process due to
your intervention. It may be an amount of
money saved by the adoption of a change
you suggested. Whatever it was, if you can
quantify it, do so.

It is easy to overlook the changes you
have been responsible for which save time
and money. Think of the following and
consider if you instigated anything similar in
your work placements:

~ Changing phone tariff or company.

~ Responding earlier so using second class
  post.

~ Delegating work to a more junior, so cheaper, member of staff.

~ Improving responses by redrafting standard letters.

~ Improving response times by suggesting the use of standard letters.

~ Putting paper records onto computer saving space and retrieval time.

~ Suggesting a better software package to improve some company function.

~ Instigating a company website.

~ Finding a cheaper supplier.

~ Bringing a new client/customer on board.

The list of possibilities is almost endless and with a little invention you can come up with something significant and relevant.

Achievements are also worth including which are not from the work place. It will be understood that you have only had a short working career so far. *

The important thing to get across is that you are one of life's achievers.

People who achieve do so in all aspects of their lives, professional, social, sporting, academic or cultural. Establish that you achieve in one field and your future employer will presume your ability to achieve in employment.

Innovations and inventions

This may sound rather pretentious, but by the time you are ready for your first post you may well have something to record under this heading. It may be a:

~ book

~ recording

~ newspaper or magazine article

~ computer programme

~ new method or technique to solve an old problem

~ device which performs a useful function,

~ page(s) on 'the net'. *

Whatever you have made, written or devised, enter it onto your CV.

Remember that most university theses are by definition inventions; the work is expected to be original and may indeed be at the cutting edge in its field. Along the way new methods or techniques may have been developed which are inventions in themselves. An innovation does not have to have a number from the patent office to be an 'invention' in this context, it just has to be original. Many inventions are conceptual, that is you may have found a new way to solve a problem or other original idea. New thought processes are valid inventions and potentially at least as valuable as novel artefacts.

Summary Points

★ If you have an employment record, what matters is what you gained from it. A brief summary of posts held and what you achieved is more valuable than a chronological listing of former jobs.

★ Make clear what you did in your work experiences; what you learned is more significant than the position you held.

★ Don't underestimate the value of your work placement. Describe what you achieved and the skills you acquired through it.

★ If you took a year out, say what you got from it. What matters is not what you did, but what the year did to you.

★ Summarise your main achievements under a separate heading.

★ Don't be reluctant to claim credit for any original work you have done. It doesn't matter if this was not directly related to this job application. It is strongly indicative of a creative mind.

4 Recording Your Educational History

I used to know from the degree title what its holder could do; now I need to be told.

Your education is presumably one of the major features of your CV. *It should occupy a prominent position in the layout*, be eye-catching and clear to the reader.

When you started to draft your CV you will have made a choice in the way you order sections between chronology and hierarchy. In the case of your education and training, it is most likely that they amount to the same thing. Your degree or diploma is both your last and highest qualification. *

* Other, more minor qualifications which you picked up on the way, can be left to the end of this section so that your school, college and university record forms a continuum.

You will also have to decide on the amount of detail to record. You have a degree so do you need to record your GCSE grades? You will name your university; is the secondary school you attended so vital?

Is this you?

- I can't remember all my GCSE grades or find the certificates. • I'm not sure that the degree I did is altogether relevant to this job. • I've done a few IT exams but I'm not sure if they're important enough to put down. • I'd rather not admit to my degree classification.

Deciding what to include

The easy answer is to *record everything that seems relevant*. The skill lies in deciding on the amount of detail that is needed. The same line on your CV could be recorded as any of the following:

GCSE	English language (B), English literature (B), history (B), art and design (B), geography (C), maths (C) science, double award (C,C), French (C)
GCSE	Nine subjects grade B-C including French
GCSEs	Nine

You might reasonably decide that by the time you have got a higher diploma or a degree your GCSE or O-level record is no longer of any significance and omit it completely.

There has to be a compromise between the over-detailed and the too sparse. For a graduate, a list of GCSE passes with grades is clearly unnecessary. Some may feel the bare 'nine' is too little. The middle ground of the number of subjects passed and the highlighting of key subjects for this application may be about right. Add subjects by name with some thought though; clearly to point out that you have GCSE French may be relevant if you have no higher language qualification and the job you want expects familiarity with a European language. It is clearly a waste of space if you have a degree in European Business Studies which entailed a year's study at a French university! *

In this light, decide on the degree of detail in which you will record all of your education.

Other questions to ask include:

~ Do you list all your A-level passes if you

did them, your Access subjects or GNVQ modules?

~ Do you itemise the units studied in a BTEC or GNVQ programme?

~ Should you name your secondary school(s)?

~ Would it help to give details of your degree profile?

Including your school and FE record

Dealing with A-levels and Access subjects

As with your GCSE record, there is little to be gained by listing these unless there is a particularly unusual one, or one very relevant to the application you are about to make, which might then be worth mentioning. Similarly, there is not much to be gained by quoting the grades you were awarded, it is enough that they were sufficient to get you onto the next rung of the ladder: your university place.

School and FE Vocational Qualifications

The broad title of the course you did is probably enough so:

GNVQ Advanced-Tourism: Merit

is quite enough detail. However, remember that most vocational courses include extra elements which might merit certification in their own right. Here are some examples which demonstrate the principle.

~ Caring programmes sometimes include a first aid course which is separately certificated or perhaps BSL (British Sign Language) signing.

~ Engineering courses may include computer aided design (CAD) qualifications.

~ Art courses also often include separate computing qualifications in Mac (Apple Macintosh) proficiency, photographic imaging or desk top publishing.

~ Leisure and Tourism courses often include certification in food hygiene or the use of databases and the Internet.

~ Almost all vocational qualifications are likely to permit extra certification in IT skills (probably through City and Guilds or the RSA) which will include use of word processors, spreadsheets, databases and perhaps the Internet and web page design. *

Your schools and colleges

There is very little point in giving details of the schools or FE colleges you attended, unless it helps you to maintain a degree of uniformity or symmetry in the design of the page. In this case you would be including the name(s) more for the presentation value than for the need to inform the reader – the thin end of a dangerous wedge?

There are clearly exceptions when there are very good reasons for including the school you attended. If you are applying for a post in the music business, you would want to mention that you had attended Cheetham's School in Manchester. If you have a similarly good reason for naming your

* If you have picked up extra skills and certificates in this way, list them as separate qualifications.

former schools, go ahead. Otherwise it hardly adds to your CV meaningfully and they can just as well be omitted.

Your university

It is expected that you will name the university at which you studied for your degree. This is usually done by adding just the name of the university at the end of your degree details: for example simply 'Leicester'. If you are a graduate of the Open University, the one word 'Open' is the accepted title.

There are a few notable exceptions to this general rule; readers may be familiar with the well known abbreviations of the Latin: Cantab. (for Cambridge) and Oxon. (Oxford).

Other abbreviations are beginning to appear for the newer universities with long names, to distinguish them from older ones in the same city. The University of Manchester Institute of Science and Technology has long been known as 'UMIST'. Similarly, The University of Central England in Birmingham is becoming known as just 'UCEB' or 'UCE Birmingham'.

Describing your degree profile

The subject that you study in your degree course is often unimportant to your suitability to do the job you are applying for, so exact details of the degree profile are then hardly important.

Applications for a graduate trainee post in recruitment would probably be equally welcome from graduates of English, psychology, computing, business studies, economics, philosophy... Each discipline would bring its own particular skills and knowledge to a management team, along with the transferable skills common to all graduates. *

However, employers *do like to have an idea what they are getting*, and for the most part they feel they do know what is involved in History or Graphic Design. Problems occur with the increasing number of degrees with titles like BA Combined Modular Studies. In this case the briefest outline of what the degree entailed would help. The modules

* To detail the degree profile would hardly be necessary.

taken may have had names like 'Experience of Creative Writing' or 'The Influence of the Renaissance in France on Tudor Dress and The Formal Garden Design in England' – but keep it simple! For instance:

BA Hon (2:2) Combined Modular Studies (English and History of Art)

There may be some aspects of your degree profile which should be explained.

A Media Studies degree may be all about artistic effect and performance or be highly technical: which was yours? This is an example of the type of degree that does need more explanation than just its title.

If your degree has 'European' in the title you have probably attained a good standard of proficiency in a European language: which one?

Vocational degrees may be accredited and so bring with them membership, or eligibility for membership, of the professional body or institute: did yours?

It is often worth describing the subject of

your main thesis, particularly if it involved research in a subject close to the heart or business of a future employer. *If your main research topic was relevant, describe it.* It scores for you twice: your future employer will be assured of your genuine interest in the subject and satisfied that they are appointing someone at the cutting edge in the industry.

Examples of education sections

Qualifications

1999   BA Fashion Design 2:1 (foundation garments)
       De Montfort University

1996   Art Foundation
       Myton College of FE

1995   A-levels: 3 inc. Art and Design

1993   GCSE 8 inc. Maths and German

RSA CLAIT
Desk top publishing levels 1 & 2

Education and Training

1999   MEng 2:2 Electrical Engineering
            UMIST

1995   ONC (eve.) General Engineering
            Otherton FE college

1988-93   Technician apprenticeship
            Box Long & Co.

Computer Aided Design course

Computer Aided Manufacture course

Full First Aid certificate

Note the effect of the choice of typeface as well as the layout of the text. You should be wary of using too extravagant a style, but you might experiment with several to find one which creates the effect you are looking for. Different typefaces also allow more (or less!) efficient use of space. *

Summary Points

* You will want to achieve both impact and readability.

★ Be selective about what you record, putting your highest qualification first.

★ Remember to include qualifications you gained at school or college which may have been secondary to your main course, but were certificated in their own right.

★ Be clear about what you studied in your degree course, the title may not be enough. Be prepared to give a brief profile of your degree if it will clarify what you did.

5 Presentation and Style

As soon as I pick up a written page I become judgemental.

Agood CV leaps from the page, grabs the attention and demands to be read. This chapter is designed to enable you to present your CV so that it will do this for you.

You will consider the overall shape of your CV, the type-faces you might use, when headings are appropriate, its ideal length and the extra information that may be worth adding at the end.

The most carefully researched and drafted CV can be ruined by poor presentation. A fairly mediocre one in terms of content can attract attention to its author beyond expectations. *

This chapter covers questions about the personal details you might, or should, include. Does it matter that you enjoy rock climbing or have a driving licence?

* It won't get you the job; it will get you into the game.

Is this you?

• *I never know whether to centre titles or not.* • *I would prefer to use a really modern typeface but wonder if I should.* • *Are headings really necessary?* • *I'm confused by hierarchies of titles.*

Getting the right format

In the traditional CV format the author's work record is usually to the fore and arranged in date order with the current or most recent position first. This *chronological* format may suit applicants with a long career record, but it may not be the best style for you.

An alternative layout you might consider is to arrange the information you want to present *hierarchically*, that is to put to the fore the things you believe are your best selling points. If you have not had very many, or very responsible, jobs you might prefer to open with your profile, key skills or your achievements in spheres other than paid employment, or even your academic record if this is the main strength of your application.

It is fairly standard practice to put your *contact details* at the top of your CV along with your name. It does not follow that your other personal details warrant the same prominence. You can safely leave your date of birth, marital status, nationality, cleanliness of driving licence, religious beliefs and preferred breakfast cereal to the end!

You will also consider the question of layout on the page. Will your address be set out as you would the address at the heading of a letter, or in linear form:

21 North Street
Bradley
Yorks
BR4 2SH

Address
21 North Street, Bradley, Yorks BR4 2SH

You have to find a compromise between consistency and the degree of flexibility which allows you to express your individuality. You will want to implant a sense of overall plan or design. *

Using headings

The standard way to make clear what you are writing about is to *give each section its own heading*. Whether this is in the best interest of clarity or aesthetics is debatable.

It probably insults the reader's intelligence to head the whole page 'curriculum vitae', but almost everyone does so, probably to prove they can spell it! Not everyone extends this logic to using the headings Name, Address, Telephone Number etc, though some do.

It is as much a question about the overall appearance of your document as it is about clarity. If you do err, try to do so on the side of clarity.

You might decide that five sections, each with its own title, is about right. These will probably include:

1 profile and/or key skills

2 education (and training)

* *Whichever order you choose to enter the information about yourself, it must be obvious at a glance to the reader what information you are giving in each section.*

3 career history

4 interests

5 additional information.

There are other headings you may want to use and these five are a useful working minimum if you intend to use titles.

Assuming that you will include some headings, you will have to choose between: upper and lower case, underlining and/or emboldening and which font to use. Experiment with some possibilities:

Education and Qualifications

Education and Qualifications

<u>Education and Qualifications</u>

EDUCATION AND QUALIFICATIONS

<u>EDUCATION AND QUALIFICATIONS</u>

<u>EDUCATION AND QUALIFICATIONS</u>

Titles are usually aligned to the left; you could experiment with centring them.

Remember that you will probably need two styles of header to permit the use of secondary titles. For example, under your

EDUCATION AND QUALIFICATIONS

You may want to use

Degree

as a secondary header, so work with titles in pairs. Does it improve the appearance of your page if one title style is underlined and the other not?

Consider whether you want all of your titles to occupy a column to themselves, or whether you will align all your text to the left as well as the titles. Look at the examples below.

PROFILE Recent Fine Art graduate (2:1 Hons), specialising in photographic techniques and digital imaging. One year's placement in advertising agency where sole responsibility was assumed for two clients. Energetic, hard-working and ambitious, determined to succeed in fashion business. Good working relations with both colleagues and clients.

<u>PROFILE</u>

Recent Fine Art graduate (2:1 Hons), specialising in photographic techniques and digital imaging. One year's placement in advertising agency where sole responsibility was assumed for two clients. Energetic, hard-working and ambitious, determined to succeed in fashion business. Good working relations with both colleagues and clients.

These are not intended to be examples of good and bad practice, they are two alternatives, one of which may appeal to you more than the other. *

* *Also consider whether you are trying to squeeze as much as you can into the available space; or that the acres of white need a large type face and wide margins to help you fill them with print.*

Including personal details

There is a host of other personal detail which you might consider giving in this section. The question is which, and why you or the reader might think them relevant. You might include:

~ Your age or date of birth

~ your marital status

~ whether you have children and how many

~ that you are a non-smoker

~ that you have a full (clean) driving licence

~ your religion

~ your nationality

~ that you have a work permit or working visa

~ your willingness to relocate if the job demands it

~ your golf handicap

~ that you are a keen squash player.

You may pick up clues as to what is worthwhile from various sources including:

~ the advertisement you are responding to

~ the extra details which came with the application form

~ the full job description

~ company policy statement or other literature they produce

~ any telephone or face-to-face contact you
   have had.

For example, the advert says that the person
appointed might be based at any one of the
company's three sites – you are 'willing to
relocate'.
   'Car allowance payable to successful
applicant': you are a car owner with five
years' experience and a clean driving record.
   The advertiser wants someone 'dynamic,
enthusiastic, self starting ...'. You give your
age, claim to be a non-smoking, regular
squash player and make sure your CV oozes
enthusiasm for life.
   'I'm sorry he's not in the office, I think he's
meeting a client at the golf club.' What was
that about a golf handicap?

Other information you should include

There are a few other sections you should
consider before finalising the outline of
your CV.

Responsibilities

You have not yet had a long enough career to have reached positions of great responsibility, *but it is worth your while highlighting what responsibilities you have accepted and discharged.* *

Under a heading Key Responsibilities you could outline briefly what positions you have held which have brought responsibility and detail how you responded.

> Responsible for the day-to-day cashflow in a large, busy office: a duty discharged without discrepancy throughout the six months of work placement.

This may just mean that you looked after the petty cash tin, but you accepted the role and fulfilled it without getting the books in a mess. By implication you not only accept responsibility, you are also methodical, accurate and honest.

Courses

You have probably been on several courses,

* At this stage in your career a selector is looking for a candidate who is willing to accept responsibility: show how you have done so thus far.

more or less related to the career you are entering. Whether they are directly relevant or not, and regardless of whether they were certificated, they may add up to a separate headed division of their own, or include them in your education section.

Don't dismiss as irrelevant courses which are not directly related to the position for which you are applying. The attendance of any course says that if something is important to you, you are willing and able to learn more about it. A key quality in a future employee.

Interests and leisure activities

If you are applying for a post as an environmental scientist, your membership of the RSPB may be relevant. If the job you want is software engineer, your judo black belt may not be so important. All activities bring benefits: improved health, better interpersonal skills or simply taking the stress out of your working life. *

* Decide which of your leisure activities are worth recording for this application, but be brief.

Summary Points

★ Choose between a hierarchical and a chronological format. It will probably suit you best to use the former, starting with your profile.

★ Decide on your policy for headings. This will help you to create a good visual impact and also to scale your CV to exactly fill one or at most two whole pages. Adjusting margins, type size and spacing will also help you to achieve this aim.

★ Include a section near the end on your personal details and circumstances which you feel are relevant.

★ Be selective in the additional information you include about yourself. Make space to include details which seem important to *this* application.

6 Writing your Covering Letter

*If your message is simple, clear and professional,
so should your letter be.*

When you send your CV to an employer, it must be accompanied by a covering letter. *This brief communication addresses your document to the right person and explains what it is and why you have sent it.*

Your letter will make clear which job application your CV is in support of; there may be several posts to be filled.

It will clarify whether you have sent your CV in response to their request, or in support of an application form. You may have sent it purely speculatively in the hope that there is a suitable vacancy for you.

This last chapter looks at how you draft and present your letter, as well as the essential details it must contain.

Is this you?

- I've prepared a great CV, but don't know how to present it. • I don't know how to word a covering letter. • I'm not sure when to use a covering letter. • I never know how to pitch the language for a business letter, or how much to say. • I'm not sure whether to include information in my covering letter that is already in my CV. • I don't know if I should say how important it is to me to get this job.

Knowing when to send a covering letter

A covering letter is an opportunity to be grasped, not a routine to follow solely for the sake of protocol. So make the most of it!

You send a covering letter with anything which is not a letter itself. You do so partly because convention demands it, but more for the common sense reasons that it allows you to address the recipient, to explain what you have sent and why, and finally to further advance your own case. Make the most of the opportunity they present. *

Getting the basics right

Before you start to write, you have to make decisions about methods, style and materials. Your CV is word processed, you might elect to demonstrate that you can also write by hand! Is the ability to write legibly likely to be an asset in the job you are applying for? Notice that some employers ask for letters to be handwritten. Conversely, is the ability to set out a formal business letter more important? It may be assumed that your CV was professionally prepared for you if you then handwrite the letter.

Invest in good quality paper and envelopes. If you use a word processor, do not be tempted to use the copy quality paper you probably use for most of your computer applications. You should also use a good quality printer, even if this means taking your disc to a centre where you can use a laser printer.

Never send covering letters on lined, punched or coloured paper. Use A4 format and avoid cards, notelets and writing paper with floral or other embellishments; all perfectly acceptable for the right occasion, but not here.

To whom are you sending this letter? Remember that it will first be read by a *person*, not a department or anonymous panel. Address your letter to that person. The personnel manager of one large company told the author:

> When I get letters addressed to "The Personnel Department" which address me as "Dear Sir or Madam" I rarely bother to read them. If they can't be bothered to find out who I am, I'm not sure that I want them working for me.

His reaction to bin these applications on a bad day may be rather extreme, but his message is clear. If you haven't been told to whom you should address your letter *find out*. This is easily done by phoning the organisation and asking the switchboard operator (if the wretched computerised switchboard will put you through to one!). If your informant tells you to send your application to 'Fiona Smedley', make sure you then ask whether Fiona should be styled 'Miss', 'Mrs' or 'Ms'. *

Before launching into the text of your letter, *title it*. It is usual to do this on one line double spaced below the opening greeting. If you are using a word processor, embolden this line. Best modern practice is neither to underline nor centre your title line, though both are commonly seen. In handwritten letters, it is correct to underline the title line; *use a ruler*. If you have been given a reference to quote, this could be quoted at the top of your letter, or may be incorporated into your title line. Hence your letter might open:

Dear Miss Smedley

Application for Sales Executive post: reference 002/FS/AB/27

Please find enclosed...

The convention for ending letters which are opened 'Dear (person's name)' is to close: 'Yours sincerely' (note, not 'your's'!). If you type or word process your letter, type your name

* *Despite the relaxation in formality over recent years, do not be tempted to open your letter 'Dear Fiona'.*

in full under this closing phrase and sign your name above the printed version. If your letter is handwritten, also write your name at the end in the same hand as the rest of the letter; it should not be necessary to hand print your name under an illegible signature.

Remember also the convention to write 'Enc.' at the foot of your letter to indicate that it was sent with an enclosure: your CV.

When opened and unfolded, your covering letter should be the top sheet of paper – face up! It should be limited to one page (if you need more space than this revise your CV). If you want to attach it to your CV, do so with a paper clip rather than a staple.

Knowing what to say

Remember that this is first and foremost a covering letter, it is primarily to *introduce your CV or application form.* This is done early in the letter with a form of words such as:

Please find attached my completed application form and a copy of my CV as requested.

Take care over your wording; is your form and CV 'attached' or are they 'enclosed' with your letter. Was your CV requested or does it need separate introduction?

I have taken this opportunity to enclose a copy of my CV which I hope you will find useful in assessing my suitability for the post.

The purpose of all this is to get an interview. *

You should indicate your willingness to be interviewed but give any times or dates when you cannot be available. Your own discretion will dictate whether you give a reason for your inability to attend interview at stated times. If you will be on holiday in this country when you are 'unavailable', it may be better not to mention it. What are your priorities? If you cannot attend any Tuesday morning for the next six weeks because you are completing a part-time course in a relevant skill, say so.

This is not a social letter. It is not the place

* The covering letter is a good vehicle to sow this seed and clarify your availability.

for general observations about the weather (however unseasonable), politics or your hopes for the health and welfare of the reader. Keep it simple and to the point.

Finally, *make it easy for your future employer to contact you to invite you for interview.* Is your telephone number included as part of your address on the CV? If not, include it in your letter. Do you do any part time work in office hours where you could you be contacted by phone? Have you got access to a fax or an e-mail address?

Selling yourself by post

Like it or not, your covering letter is part of the overall impression you make as an applicant. *Make this work to your advantage* and use the letter as a self marketing tool by adding:

~ the reasons why your application should be accepted

~ details about yourself not in your CV or in your CV and worth highlighting.

One or perhaps two paragraphs of your letter could be devoted to strengthening your claim for appointment, or at least to making you more worthy of an interview.

You might describe how the job description closely mirrors your ideal job. *Say why this is and what strengths, interests, skills or experiences you have which make the post ideal for you (and you for the post).*

Case study

Tom had just finished his geography degree and saw a job advertised for a statistician to work for a county council in their education department. His degree thesis had been a survey of school exam results, partly stemming from his access to local results: both of his parents were teachers, though in contrasting parts of the city. He applied for the job and described his thesis in the covering letter, thus demonstrating his existing interest in this work, a basis in the necessary skills and a little relevant experience. His degree was neither in statistics nor computing, but he got the job.

Including other information

If you have read Chapter 1 you will have done an inventory of your own strengths. Apply them to the job description of the post you are applying for. Which are the most telling overlaps or the closest matches? Don't just rely on the selector noticing them in your CV, point them out as well in this part of your letter. *

Consider some of the following possibilities.

You have not included your *marital status* in your CV. This job will necessitate moving from base to base over the first few years of the appointment. Might it help to point out that you are single, unattached and prepared to be mobile?

The job advertisement warned of the necessity to work outdoors in all weathers. Suddenly your favourite pastime, hill-walking in the Lake District, is well worth a mention in your covering letter.

More often something which is already in your CV is worth expanding upon.

The successful applicant will get a

* Your CV cannot possibly contain every detail about you. Are there any details which might be germane to this application which are not in your CV?

company car. Your CV mentions full clean driving licence. Is this the time to add that you have driven your own car for four years with neither accident nor insurance claim?

Your CV includes a period of work experience with a named company. Now may be the time to expand on this to point out the company you were with is in the same business as the firm you are now applying to, that you were happy and successful in that environment and got many useful ideas during your time with them.

Well written, the self advocacy section of your letter can carry powerful images which will encourage the selector to take a closer look at you – *and invite you to interview.*

Summary Points

★ When you send anything through the post, which is not itself a letter, it should be introduced by a covering letter. This includes your CV and application forms. Address your letter to the intended recipient by name if at all possible unless instructed otherwise.

★ Your covering letter should be formally written on good quality paper, professional in appearance and containing a title line.

★ Your covering letter should be brief and formal. Use it to introduce your CV and/or application form. Beyond this you may wish to say where you saw the job advertised and to clarify your availability for interview. If you feel you need to add further important details, it is your CV which needs attention.

★ You might use your letter to strengthen your application, pointing out why you are suitable for the post by detailing particular strengths of your application. You will be emphasising information already included in your CV, or the application form if you have completed one.

A CV Checklist

1 The visual impact must be good, it must ask to be read.

2 Messages must be clear and simple, the reader should not have to read between the lines.

3 Use strong 'action' words and avoid the use of 'I', 'my', etc.

4 List qualifications and previous jobs in order, most recent (or current) first.

5 Your first draft should err on the side of too much detail, it's easier to edit down than to pad out and the result will be crisper for it.

6 Give yourself time to do the job properly.

7 Think of your CV as advertiser's copy, for your own services.

8 This is not the place for modesty. If you don't describe how good you are, who will?

9 Emphasise your achievements to date, quantified if possible.

10 Do not include referees' details, supply these separately if and when asked.

11 Use good quality paper and printer.

12 Take time to compose a good covering letter addressed to the person to receive it by name, unless told otherwise.